CAKE POPS

HOLIDAYS *by Bakerella*

BY ANGIE DUDLEY

CHRONICLE BOOKS

SAN FRANCISCO

DEDICATION

For my mom who gave
me the gift of life twice.
You are my angel.
I love you.

For my dad who I miss
dearly and who would
have been so proud of
this book.

ACKNOWLEDGMENTS

To all the readers of Bakerella.com—
Thank you for visiting the site, sharing
your own cake pops and making me smile
every day. Your stories and successes
mean more than I can say. I hope you
enjoy this holiday book and that it
helps you bring as much happiness to
everyone in your lives as you have
brought to mine.

A huge thank you to everyone at Chronicle
Books, including the wonderful team
that helped make this book happen—
Amy Treadwell, my editor; Emily Dubin,
art director; Marina Sauri, designer;
Leigh Saffold, managing editor; Tera Killip,
production coordinator; Michael Melby;
David Hawk; and especially Peter Perez,
for being a friend along the way. It's been
a huge pleasure working with all of you.

My family and friends—This has been a
challenging year with my health and hos-
pital stays. I love you so much and thank
you for being there with me during all of
the ups and downs. And Julie, thank you
for being a sweet friend and letting me
make a mess in your kitchen.

To the transplant team, nurses, and staff
at Emory and the Transplant Clinic—I'm
so grateful for your talent and everything
you do. I want to thank you for taking
such wonderful care of me and my mom.
You helped make it possible for me to
create this book, but most important, for
me and my mom to have more holidays
together. Thank you.

Library of Congress
Cataloging-in-Publication
Data available.

ISBN 978-1-4521-1116-2

Manufactured in China

Designed by Marina Saurí

10 9 8 7 6 5 4 3 2 1

Chronicle Books LLC
680 Second Street
San Francisco, California 94107
www.chroniclebooks.com

Contents

INTRODUCTION 5

GETTING STARTED WITH CAKE POPS 7

Basic Cake Pops 9

Cake & Frosting Recipes 15

Tools & Techniques 18

Displaying & Gifting 30

HOLIDAY CAKE POP PROJECTS 33

Gingerheads 35

Welcoming Wreaths 37

Simple Snowflakes 41

Stuffed Stockings 42

Jingle Bells 45

Peppermint Pops 46

Polar Bears 49

Sweet Soldiers 51

Pretty Presents 55

Red-Nosed Reindeer 57

Santas 58

Freckled Elves 61

Bright Lights 65

Ornaments 67

Cheery Christmas Trees 69

Gingerbread Houses 71

Delightful Dreidels 75

Colorful Cardinals 77

Frosty Friends 79

Jolly Holly 83

Festive Pets 85

Snow Globes 87

RESOURCES 90

CAKE POP PROJECTS PHOTO INDEX 92

INDEX 93

Introduction

My first book, *Cake Pops*, introduced you to the wonderful world of creative little cakes on a stick. These tiny, candy-covered confections are a mixture of crumbled cake and frosting that you can shape and decorate for any occasion. And so many of you did just that—you made cake pops and unleashed your creativity, spreading delight wherever you shared your treats and maybe even surprising yourself along the way with your talent.

Cake pops have become an international phenomenon since I posted my first designs on my website in 2008. I have enjoyed all the creations you've shared with me, and the love and excitement you possess for making them. I can't tell you how happy it makes me to know that cake pops have found a special place in the hearts of so many.

That's why I wanted to do this book featuring more cake pop designs, this time focused on the holiday season, that you can share with your friends and family.

Maybe you've made cake pops before. Maybe you are ready to try them for the very first time. Either way, winter holidays are the most festive times to bake and decorate, and cake pops let you do both. But, more importantly, cake pops will bring smiles to everyone you share them with.

Let the holiday cheer begin.

Getting Started with Cake Pops

❋

Cake pops are crumbled cake mixed with frosting and rolled into bite-size balls, which are dipped in candy coating and served lollipop-style on a stick. They are the basis of all the projects in this book and a canvas for your creativity. Once you know how to make them, you will have the skills to create amazing tiny treats that will impress you and anyone you give them to.

You can make cake pops with just about any cake and frosting you like, but I usually tell people to learn how to make them using purchased mixes and frostings to start. Cakes made from box mixes provide consistent results and crumble beautifully, and they go together quickly and easily, allowing you to focus on the design and technique as you learn.

Read through the following pages for easy instructions and helpful information to get you started making your very own cake pops.

Basic Cake Pops

Once you know how to make a basic cake pop, it's easy to start making the projects in this book or create your own designs.

YOU'LL NEED

18.25-oz (520-g) box cake mix

9-by-13-in (23-by-33-cm) cake pan

Two baking sheets

Wax paper

Large mixing bowl

16-oz (455-g) container ready-made frosting

Large metal spoon

Plastic wrap

48 oz (1.4 kg) candy coating

Deep, microwave-safe plastic bowl

48 lollipop sticks

Styrofoam block

MAKES 48 CAKE POPS

1. Bake the cake as directed on the box, using the 9-by-13-in (23-by-33-cm) cake pan. Let cool completely.

2. Once the cake has cooled, get organized and set aside plenty of time (a couple of hours) to crumble, roll, and dip 4 dozen cake pops. Line the baking sheets with wax paper.

3. Crumble the cooled cake into the large bowl. You should not see any big pieces of cake.

4. Add up to three-quarters of the container of frosting to the bowl. (You will not need the remaining frosting. Save it in the refrigerator for a later use.) Mix it into the crumbled cake, using the back of a large metal spoon, until thoroughly combined. If you use the entire container, the cake balls will be too moist.

5. The mixture should be moist enough to roll into 1 ½-in (4-cm) balls and still hold a round shape. After rolling the cake balls by hand, place them on the prepared baking sheets and let them rest for about 20 minutes before chilling.

Continued

6. Cover with plastic wrap and chill for several hours in the refrigerator, or place them in the freezer for about 15 minutes. You want the balls to be firm but not frozen.

7. Place the candy coating in the deep microwave-safe bowl. These bowls make it easier to cover the cake balls completely with candy coating while holding the bowl and without burning your fingers. The coating should be about 3 in (7.5 cm) deep for easier dipping. I usually work with about 16 oz (455 g) of coating at a time.

8. Melt the candy coating, following the instructions on the package. Microwave on medium power for 30 seconds at a time, stirring with a spoon between each interval. You can also use a double boiler. Either way, make sure you do not overheat the coating. See "Working with Candy Coating," page 20, for more candy coating basics.

9. Now you're ready to dip. Take a few cake balls out of the refrigerator or freezer to work with, keeping the rest chilled. If they're in the freezer, transfer the rest of the balls to the refrigerator at this point so they stay firm but do not freeze.

10. One at a time, dip about ½ in (12 mm) of the tip of a lollipop stick into the melted candy coating, and then insert the lollipop stick straight into a cake ball, pushing it no more than halfway through.

11. Holding the lollipop stick with cake ball attached, dip the entire cake ball into the melted candy coating until it is completely covered, and remove it in one motion. Make sure the coating meets at the base of the lollipop stick. This helps secure the cake ball to the stick when the coating sets. The object is to completely cover the cake ball and remove it without submerging it in the coating more than once. A small, deep plastic bowl is very helpful during this step. If you do resubmerge the cake pop, the weight of the candy coating can pull on the cake ball and cause it to get stuck in the coating.

12. The thinner the consistency of your coating, the easier it will be to coat the cake pops. If you find that your coating is too thick, add some vegetable oil or paramount crystals to help thin it and make the coating more fluid.

Continued

13. When you remove the cake pop from the candy coating, some excess coating may start to drip. Hold the cake pop in one hand and use the other to gently tap the first wrist. Rotate the lollipop stick if necessary to allow the excess coating to fall off evenly, so one side doesn't get heavier than the other. If you didn't completely dunk the cake pop, this method of tapping and rotating generally takes care of that. The coating will slowly slide down the surface of the cake ball until it reaches the lollipop stick.

14. If too much coating surrounds the base of the lollipop stick, you can wipe the excess off with your finger. Simply place your finger on the stick right under the cake ball and rotate the pop, allowing any excess coating to fall off and back into the bowl of coating. When most of the excess coating has fallen off and it is no longer dripping, stick the cake pop into the Styrofoam block.

15. Repeat with the remaining cake balls and let the pops dry completely in the Styrofoam block.

16. Enjoy!

⊹ TIPS ⊱

- Make the cake the day before, and let it cool overnight.

- Use a toothpick to encourage the coating to cover any small exposed areas or to make sure it surrounds the lollipop stick.

- Make sure the cake balls are chilled and firm when you dip them. If they are room temperature, they are likely to fall off the lollipop sticks into the melted candy coating. You can always return them to the freezer for a few minutes to quickly firm up again.

- Experiment with different colors of candy coating and sprinkles.

- You can also make cake pops into different shapes. Just roll them into balls, place in the freezer or refrigerator to firm and mold into your desired shape. See page 19 for more on making shapes.

- Poke holes in the Styrofoam block before you start dipping. Just use one of the lollipop sticks to make holes about 2 in (5 cm) apart.

STORING CAKE POPS

Cake pops made with a cake mix and ready-made frosting can be stored in an airtight container on the counter for several days. If you wrap them individually in treat bags tied with ribbon, they can stand in a Styrofoam block or cake pop stand.

Cake pops made with homemade ingredients that are perishable, such as cream cheese frosting, should be stored in the refrigerator, either in an airtight container or wrapped in treat bags.

Note: Candy coating manufacturers do not recommend storing the candy coating wafers in the refrigerator or freezer, but I have had success storing the finished coated cake pops by wrapping them in individual treat bags tied with a ribbon and placing them in an airtight container in the freezer.

TROUBLESHOOTING

You followed all the directions but still need a little more help. Take a look at some of the following scenarios to see if you can find the answer to your cake pop questions.

YOUR CAKE IS TOO MOIST AND WILL NOT HOLD ITS SHAPE WHEN ROLLED INTO A BALL. You probably used too much frosting in proportion to cake. Add more cake to balance it out. Try crumbling in a few store-bought cupcakes, minus the frosting.

YOUR COATING WON'T COVER THE CAKE BALL SMOOTHLY. Make sure the balls are firm and not frozen. Frozen cake balls mixed with hot candy coating will cause the coating to start to set too quickly, often before the cake ball can be coated properly. If your cake balls are chilled properly and the coating still won't cover them smoothly, read through the dipping method again (see page 22) for

tips. Also make sure the coating is thin enough to dip easily.

YOU CAN'T FIND CANDY COATING. Candy coating is available in most craft stores, cake-supply stores, and online, but if you are unable to find any in your area, try melting regular chocolate, and use shortening or paramount crystals to make it easier to dip. This alternative is best used when making cake balls, because chocolate does not set as hard as candy coating does, making it less suitable for supporting cake pops on their sticks.

YOU MADE CAKE POPS AND THE COATING CRACKED. You may have rolled the cake balls too tightly. And if placed in the freezer for too long, the cake may have tried to expand, resulting in a crack in the coating. Don't worry; they won't fall off the stick if they've been secured by coating at the base. And you can even dip them a second time to fix it up or drizzle or decorate in a way to disguise the crack. You can also conceal the crack, by using a toothpick to fill in the opening with melted candy coating and then wipe off any excess. The crack will virtually disappear when the coating dries. It can help to give them time to rest and expand before you place them in the fridge or freezer for the first time—leave them out for about 20 minutes.

YOUR CANDY COATING IS TOO THICK. Don't turn up the heat. Making the candy coating hotter doesn't make it thinner. When you are melting the coating, do so slowly and on a low temperature. If your coating is melted and is still too thick, add vegetable oil, shortening, or paramount crystals to the melted coating until it is thin enough to work with. If you have to reheat it to melt the shortening or crystals, do so at a low heat.

YOUR CAKE POPS KEEP FALLING OFF THE STICKS. Make sure the shaped cake balls are firm but not frozen when you dip them. If they start to get too soft, just return them to the freezer for a few minutes to firm them up again. Make sure the coating is thin enough to dip and remove in one motion so you are not tempted to stir the cake pops in the coating. Also make sure that you don't insert sticks more than halfway through the cake pops. Finally, check that the coating surrounds the cake ball at the base where the lollipop stick is inserted. Use a toothpick if necessary to direct the coating around the base of the stick.

CAKE CRUMBS ARE GETTING MIXED IN WITH THE CANDY COATING. The cake balls may not be firm enough. Chill them for a little longer before dipping. If you use dark-colored cake, such as chocolate or red velvet, with lighter-colored candy coatings, some crumbs may show up anyway. If so, just redip them a second time in a new batch of melted candy coating.

YOU CAN SEE YOUR CAKE THROUGH THE CANDY COATING. When you use dark-colored cake and white or light-colored candy coatings, this can happen. To make the coating completely opaque, you can dip the cake balls a second time. Let the first coat dry before you dip again.

YOUR CANDY COATING HAS A GRAYISH, FILMY-LOOKING SURFACE. This is most likely what is called "bloom" and can be caused by improper storage of candy coating or changes in temperature when shipping. To avoid bloom, store your coatings properly in a cool, dry place away from direct heat or sunlight, and avoid temperature changes. When purchasing candy coating from a store, pick out the package with the least amount of bloom, to get off to a good start. FYI: Coatings affected by bloom may not be as pretty, but they are still safe to eat.

Cake & Frosting Recipes

Learning to make cake pops using a box cake mix and ready-made frosting is easy and the results are dependable. There's no need to wonder if your homemade cake recipe makes the right amount of cake to accompany your homemade frosting recipe. The proportions are pretty perfect—cake mixes are consistent that way. But if you want to branch out beyond the box, here are a few basic recipes to get you started. Or feel free to experiment with your own cake and frosting recipes.

These recipes yield about 60 cake pops. Use them with one of the frosting recipes in this chapter to maintain a good cake-to-frosting ratio when making cake balls.

YELLOW CAKE

Makes one 9-by-13-in (23-by-33-cm) cake

3 cups (380 g) all-purpose flour (spooned and leveled)

2 tsp baking powder

½ tsp salt

1 cup (225 g) unsalted butter, at room temperature

2 cups (400 g) sugar

4 large eggs, at room temperature

2 tsp vanilla extract

1 cup (240 ml) whole milk, at room temperature

Preheat the oven to 350°F (180°C/gas 4). Grease and flour a 9-by-13-in (23-by-33-cm) cake pan.

In a medium bowl, whisk together the flour, baking powder, and salt. Set aside.

In a large bowl, cream the butter and sugar with a mixer for 5 minutes, or until light and fluffy.

Add the eggs, one at a time, to the creamed sugar and butter, mixing until just combined. Scrape down the sides of the bowl after each addition. Add the vanilla and mix until combined.

Beat in the flour mixture to the butter mixture one-third at a time, alternating with the milk in 2 additions. (You'll begin and end with the flour mixture.)

Spread the batter (it will be thick) evenly into the prepared pan and bake for 35 to 40 minutes, or until a toothpick inserted into the center comes out clean.

Let the cake cool completely before crumbling for cake balls (see page 18).

CHOCOLATE CAKE

Makes one 9-by-13-in (23-by-33-cm) cake

2 ½ cups (315 g) all-purpose flour (spooned and leveled)

1 cup (100 g) unsweetened cocoa powder

2 tsp baking powder

1 tsp baking soda

½ tsp salt

1 cup (225 g) unsalted butter, at room temperature

2 cups (400 g) sugar

3 large eggs, at room temperature

1 tsp vanilla extract

1 ½ cups (360 ml) whole milk, at room temperature

Preheat the oven to 350°F (180°C/gas 4). Grease and flour a 9-by-13-in (23-by-33-cm) cake pan.

In a large bowl, whisk together the flour, cocoa powder, baking powder, baking soda, and salt. Set aside.

Cream the butter and sugar with a mixer for 5 minutes, or until light and fluffy.

Add the eggs, one at a time, to the creamed sugar and butter, mixing until just combined. Scrape down the sides of the bowl after each addition. Add the vanilla and mix until combined.

Beat in the flour mixture to the butter mixture one-third at a time, alternating with the milk in 2 additions. (You'll begin and end with the flour mixture.)

Spread the batter (it will be thick) evenly into the prepared pan and bake for 35 to 40 minutes, or until a toothpick inserted into the center comes out clean.

Let the cake cool completely before crumbling for cake balls (see page 18).

RED VELVET CAKE

Makes one 9-by-13-in (23-by-33-cm) cake

2 ½ cups (315 g) all-purpose flour

2 cups (400 g) sugar

1 tbsp unsweetened cocoa powder

1 tsp baking soda

½ tsp salt

2 large eggs

1 cup (240 ml) vegetable oil

1 cup (240 ml) buttermilk

1 tbsp white vinegar

1 tsp vanilla extract

2 tbsp red food coloring

Preheat the oven to 350°F (180°C/gas 4). Grease and flour a 9-by-13-in (23-by-33-cm) cake pan.

In a large bowl, whisk together the flour, sugar, cocoa powder, baking soda, and salt. Set aside.

Lightly stir eggs in a bowl with a wire whisk. Add the oil, buttermilk, vinegar, vanilla extract, and food color and whisk until blended. Add the wet ingredients to the dry ingredients and beat with a mixer on medium-high for about a minute or until completely combined.

Pour into the baking pan. Drop the pan on the counter a few times to release any air bubbles. Bake for about 35 minutes, or until a toothpick inserted comes out clean.

BUTTERCREAM FROSTING

3/4 cup (170 g) butter, at room temperature

1 tsp vanilla extract

3 cups (300 g) confectioners' sugar

1 to 2 tsp milk, if needed

Cream the butter and vanilla with a mixer until combined.

Add the sugar to the creamed mixture in two or three batches, scraping down the sides of the bowl after each addition. Mix until combined.

It needed, add 1 or 2 teaspoons of milk to make the frosting creamier.

For chocolate buttercream: Add 1/3 cup unsweetened cocoa powder before adding milk and mix until combined.

CREAM CHEESE FROSTING

6 tbsp (85 g) butter, at room temperature

6 oz (170 g) cream cheese, at room temperature

1 tsp vanilla extract

3 cups (300 g) confectioners' sugar

Cream the butter and cream cheese with a mixer until combined.

Add the vanilla and mix until combined.

Add the sugar to the creamed mixture in two or three batches, scraping down the sides of the bowl after each addition.

For chocolate cream cheese frosting: Add 1/3 cup unsweetened cocoa powder at the end and mix until combined.

Tools & Techniques

GETTING STARTED

The techniques involved in making cake pops are simple, but there are a lot of moving parts, so it's important to get organized before you begin. Setting up your tools and ingredients will save you a lot of time and unnecessary frustration; you don't want to be counting out candies for decorating after you've begun dipping the pops!

Read through a recipe and assemble the items you need. Take out all your ingredients and put them within easy reach. Sprinkles and candies can go in small dishes, and lollipop sticks can stand in a small glass.

You can also make the cake the night before and let it cool. Then your time the next day can be devoted to rolling the balls and dipping and decorating.

Take some time and read through the following pages before you begin a cake pop project, and you'll be on your way to becoming a pop star. *For more cake pops designs from the readers of Bakerella. com, visit www.bakerella.com/pop-stars.*

CRUMBLING YOUR CAKE AND MIXING THE BASE

There are two main ways to crumble your cake and prepare it to be combined with frosting. The first, and handiest, is to just use, well, your hands. This method works great with cakes from box mixes, which have a texture that crumbles easily. Just cut a baked 9-by-13-in (23-by-33-cm) cake into four equal sections. Remove a section from the pan, break it in half, and rub the two pieces together over a large bowl, making sure to crumble any big pieces that fall off. You can also use a fork to break

any larger pieces of cake apart. Repeat with each section until the entire cake is rendered into fine, uniform crumbs. If you have large pieces mixed in, the cake balls may turn out lumpy and bumpy and will cause your candy coating to look uneven when you dip.

If you bake a cake from scratch, you can still crumble it using your hands. But because the texture of scratch cakes can vary so much, it may be easier to just toss small sections of the cake into a food processor. This will ensure that the texture is fine enough.

- Are 4 dozen cake pops too many? You can make as few as a dozen at a time. Each quarter section of cake yields about 12 cake pops. Remember to adjust the amount of frosting accordingly. Just freeze the extra cake quarter sections and save for later use.

- When using light-colored cakes, remove any brown edges before crumbling to avoid brown specks in your cake balls. Just remember if you are crumbling less cake, you will need less frosting.

- Mix one quarter of a 9-by-13-in cake, or about 3 cups fine cake crumbs, with ¼ cup frosting for 12 pops.

Add the frosting—about 1 cup (340 g) is what you need for a 9-by-13-in (23-by-33-cm) cake (yields around 12 cups of fine cake crumbs)—and mix with a large spoon until the crumbs absorb the frosting and it disappears into the cake. Using the back of your spoon is a quick way to make sure the two are thoroughly combined.

CREATING SHAPES

Crumbled cake mixed with frosting is easily rolled by hand into round balls. That same pliability opens a whole other range of possibilities for sweet creations, by molding the base into oval, square, or triangular shapes. Subtle changes in shape can turn a Christmas tree into Christmas light. And even if you don't change the shape at all, you'll find that decorating with different add-ons and candies can transform a basic round shape into endless designs.

Here's a guide to the most commonly used shapes from the ideas in this book.

Round: Red-Nosed Reindeer, Jingle Bells, Jolly Holly, Simple Snowflakes, Santas, Ornaments

Oval: Freckled Elves

Rectangular: Delightful Dreidels, Gingerbread Houses, Pretty Presents

Rounded triangles/cones: Cheery Christmas Trees, Bright Lights

Cookie-cutter shapes: Gingerheads

Pattles: Peppermint Pops

Rings: Welcoming Wreaths

Crescents: Colorful Cardinals

Before custom shaping, make round cake balls to ensure you'll end up with the desired number. If you start shaping right away, you may end up with shapes that are too big or too small.

It's helpful to place the cake balls in the freezer for a few minutes to firm up before reshaping them. Don't roll the cake balls too tightly. They may try to expand after coating, which can cause the coating to crack.

You can use wax paper to aid in shaping straight sides on the balls. For example, to shape a square, take a cake ball and slide each side on a wax paper–covered baking sheet to create a flat surface. Rotate and repeat until you have shaped a square. For an even more defined shape, use the flat side of a cookie cutter or knife to cut off any rounded excess and flatten the sides.

WORKING WITH CANDY COATING

Candy coating, also referred to as candy wafers, compound coatings, confectionery coating, chocolate bark, bark coating, and candy melts, is a mainstay of candy making. It may be used for dipping or poured into candy molds or into squeeze bottles for piping or drizzling. Candy coating

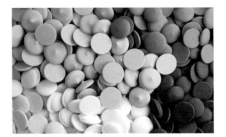

comes in a variety of colors and flavors. It is easy to use and doesn't require tempering, as chocolate does. Just melt and use.

It doesn't hurt to keep an extra bag of candy coating in the color you are using on hand just in case you run short. You can always use it for a future project if it turns out you don't need it.

Store candy coating in a cool, dry place until ready to use. Do not store in the refrigerator or freezer. If stored properly, leftover candy coatings can even be remelted and used again.

MELTING METHODS To use candy coating, simply melt the amount you need and

you're ready to go. Rather than melting all the candy coating at once, I usually work with about 16 oz (455 g) at a time. Try one of the following methods to find the one that appeals to you most.

Microwave: Melt the candy coating in a small, deep, microwave-safe bowl. Microwave on medium power in 30-second intervals, stirring in between. Repeat until the coating is completely melted. When you first stir, the coating will still be firm. That's okay; just keep repeating, making sure not to overheat the coating. In addition, be sure not to let any water mix with the coating.

Double boiler: I don't usually use this method because most of the time I melt more than one color of candy coating, for which it's easier to use the microwave and work with a number of smaller bowls. However, if you are using one color, the double boiler method is a great alternative. Fill the bottom section of a double boiler with water and bring to a simmer. Remove it from the heat and place candy coating in the top section. Stir continuously until completely melted and smooth.

Warming tray: A warming tray allows you to use several oven-safe bowls at one time. Make sure they are small and deep enough for dipping. Turn the tray on low and you will be able to keep multiple colors melted. It is also helpful when working with cake pops that require a lot of sprinkles to be attached for the design. The warming tray will keep the coating melted so you can work at your own pace without having to reheat the coating often.

THINNING CANDY COATING Working with candy coating can be lots of fun, but only if it is working with you. Sometimes the coating is too thick, making it more difficult to dip the cake pops. An easy way to thin the coating is to use a product called paramount crystals, adding a few pieces to the coating. Stir until melted and fluid. You can also use regular shortening or even vegetable oil as an alternative. Start by adding just a teaspoon. Stir in until melted. Add more as needed until

the coating is fluid enough to work with easily. Never use water to thin candy coating. It will ruin the coating properties and you will have to start all over again.

COLORING CANDY COATING Although candy coating comes in a variety of basic colors, sometimes you need to tint your own to get just the right shade. Tinting white candy coating is also a great alternative if you need only a small amount of one color and don't want to buy a whole package of coating. Add a few drops of candy coloring to start. Add more color, a few drops at a time, until you achieve the shade you desire. If you add too much color, you can lighten it by adding more white candy coating.

Make sure to use oil-based candy coloring and not regular food coloring, which contains water. Food coloring will ruin the coating.

ADDING FLAVORINGS Besides adding color to your candy coating, you can also flavor it with candy oils. These intense flavorings are stronger than the regular

flavorings and extracts you'll find in the baking section of the grocery store. You need to use only a small amount. Some examples of flavors that would be fun for the holidays are amaretto, cinnamon, eggnog, coffee, nutmeg, and peppermint. Other examples of oils that are fun to add any time of year are bubblegum, cotton candy, cola, marshmallow, lavender, and root beer. And that's just the tip of the icing.

USING CHOCOLATE AS A COATING SUBSTITUTE Regular chocolate can be used as a substitute for candy coating, but keep in mind that the coatings are made to do just that—coat. Baking chocolate and morsels will cover the cake balls but will not harden in the same way that candy coating will. Therefore, this alternative is best when making cake balls instead of cake pops, because the pops need a hard coating to give them extra stability on the sticks. You may also need to thin chocolate with shortening or paramount crystals to make it more fluid.

CANDY COATING COLORS In addition to candy coating flavors such as chocolate and peanut butter, vanilla candy coating is available in a rainbow of colors, like red, green, blue, pink, orange, yellow, peach, purple, and even black.

You can also combine candy coating colors to achieve even more shades. For instance, you can lighten any color by adding white candy melts or mix shades to create different colors, which I do for Santa and Freckled Elves pops to create flesh tones.

Some candy coating colors are also available in mint flavor, including chocolate, white, and pink.

DIPPING CAKE POPS The question I have been asked the most is "How do you get your coating so smooth?" Well, it's really simple.

I use small bowls of melted candy coating about 3 in (7.5 cm) deep. Make sure the coating is thin enough to dip and

DIPPING DO'S & DON'TS

- Do use a bowl deep enough to dip your cake pops and remove them in one motion.

- Don't get any water in your candy coating.

- Do keep a dry dish towel or paper towels nearby to wipe off your hands.

- Don't overheat your candy coating.

- Do use shortening or paramount crystals to thin coating that is too thick.

- Don't use regular food coloring to tint candy coating.

- Do use special candy coloring to tint it.

- Don't push lollipop sticks more than halfway through the cake ball.

- Do dip the sticks in melted coating before you insert them into cake pops.

- Don't dip frozen cake balls. Firm, yes. Frozen, no.

- Do have a lot of fun.

remove easily. You can use paramount crystals, shortening, or even vegetable oil to thin coatings. Make sure your coating is deep enough to allow you to completely submerge the firmed cake pop.

Small, narrow, and deep microwave-safe plastic bowls are best so you can hold the bowl easily without burning any fingers. Glass bowls retain heat and can get too hot or continue to heat the coating. Dip about 1/2 in (12 mm) of the tip of a lollipop stick into the melted coating to help "glue" it into the cake. Insert the lollipop stick into a cake ball, pushing it no more than half-way through.

Dip the cake pop once in the melted coating, submerging the cake ball completely, and remove it in one motion. If the coating is too thick, gently tap off any excess: Hold it over the bowl in your left hand, and tap your left wrist gently with your right hand. If you use the hand holding the cake pop to shake off excess coating, the force of the movement will be too strong and could cause the cake ball to loosen or fly off the lollipop stick. Tapping the wrist holding the cake pop absorbs some of the impact. The excess coating will fall off, but you will need to rotate the lollipop stick so the coating doesn't build up on one side, making it too heavy on that side. If too much coating starts to build up at the base of the stick, simply use your finger to wipe it off, spinning the lollipop stick at the same time. This can

happen if the coating is too thin or too hot. It's not as hard as it sounds; it just takes a little practice.

Complete instructions for cake pops are on page 9.

USING CANDY COATING AS GLUE After your cake pops are coated and dry, you can use any remaining candy coating left in your dipping bowl as glue. Apply it to candy or sprinkles with a toothpick and attach them to the cake pop. You can also apply it to a coated, dry cake ball and then place the add-on in position. Use a tiny amount of coating to attach the smallest items, such as sprinkles. Use a slightly larger amount for bigger add-ons, such as M&M's or candy necklace pieces. When the coating dries, the add-on will be attached, or "glued" on. If the coating in the bowl has dried, simply heat it again to melt it.

MAIN INGREDIENTS

Here's a handy list of edible ingredients used in making cake pops.

Cake: Cake mixes, homemade cakes, and store-bought cakes can all be used to create cake pops. Avoid using cakes that are extremely moist or that contain fruit, because when combined with frosting, the texture can become, for lack of a better word, gooey.

Candy coating: Coatings are widely available in disc form but are also available in blocks. Wilton and Make 'n Mold are popular brands that you can find in craft stores and even online. Merckens is another brand that is available online and in cake supply stores. Grocery stores, such as Kroger, even carry their own brand of candy coating. Be aware that when ordering candy coating online during the summer months, your coating can arrive already melted. Don't worry, though; you can still use it.

Candy coloring: Wilton and Chefmaster are two makers of candy coloring. These colorings are oil based and do not contain water. Never use regular food coloring, which does contain water, as it will ruin your candy coating.

Candy-flavoring oils: Use candy-flavoring oils to add flavor to candy coatings. They are not a necessity by any means, but you may want to experiment for fun.

Candy writers: Try these handy tubes of colored candy coating for smaller jobs. Just heat, following the directions on the package, and use right out of the tube. They're quick, easy, and definitely not messy. Colors include black, brown, red, white, yellow, green, orange, and pink, to name a few.

Cocoa butter: Plain cocoa butter is a pale-yellow vegetable fat that comes in a solid state, but can be melted and used to help thin candy coating. It can also be tinted with powdered food colors and used to paint on the surface of chocolate.

Cocoa butter also comes pre-colored in bottles. To use, melt in the microwave on low in 15-second increments or in a warm water bath, shake well and pour out of the bottle. You can paint directly on finished cake pops using a small brush.

Edible add-ons: Sprinkles, candies, nuts, and cookies are fun ways to transform plain cake pops into party pops for every occasion.

Edible-ink pens: Dot your eyes! Edible-ink pens are an excellent tool to have on hand if you decide to add personality to your cake pops. They are quick and easy. Use them to draw eyes, mouths, eyelashes, and other details. Americolor Gourmet Writer pens come in colors like black, brown, pink, red, blue, and more. You can buy a whole set or just black to suit your need.

Use edible-ink pens carefully. If you press down too hard when drawing on the candy coating, residue from the candy will build up on the tip, making the pens difficult to

use. So use a very light touch. Imagine the pen as a paintbrush and the pops as your canvas. When dotting eyes on sprinkles, though, you'll need to press a little harder.

Edible spray: Add a little sparkle to your pops with edible metallic spray. It comes in colors like gold, silver, and non-metallic colors, too.

Frosting: You can combine any flavor frosting with any flavor cake you like. Homemade frostings also work. If using frosting with perishable ingredients, such as cream cheese, make sure you store finished treats in the refrigerator.

If using ready-made frosting, avoid the whipped varieties.

Luster dust: You can also use luster dust, which comes in a wide array of shimmery colors. Just stir together a small amount of dust and a few drops of clear extract to transform it into a liquid and paint it on your pops or candy.

Paramount crystals: This product is ideal for thinning candy coating. It's available online from cake- and candy-supply websites and cake-supply stores. Shortening and even vegetable oil are also acceptable alternatives. Start by adding about a teaspoon per pound of coating until the coating is fluid enough to dip.

EQUIPMENT

You can make sensational treats with these simple tools.

Baking sheets: 12-by-18-in (30.5-by-46-cm) rimmed baking sheets are large enough to hold 48 cake balls. However, smaller rimmed baking sheets are easy to slide in and out of the freezer or refrigerator—especially if you have a side-by-side model.

Cake pan: Use a 9-by-13-in (23-by-33-cm) cake pan. Buy one with a lid—it will come in handy if you choose to bake the cake the night before you dip and decorate.

Candy molds: These are sold in hundreds of shapes and sizes. They can aid in making perfect shapes to accessorize your cake pops. For example, cordial cup molds work great for the Sweet Soldiers' hats (page 51). Familiarize yourself with what's available and watch your creativity skyrocket.

Candy gloves: These are great to have on hand. When holding items made of candy coating, like the Sweet Soldiers' hats (page 51), your body heat can start to make impressions in the coating. Candy gloves can help prevent this.

Cookie cutters: Cookie cutters can come in handy when making cake pop shapes. Small circle cutters will come in handy for the Gingerheads (page 35) and Peppermint Pops (page 46). If you have small cutters for any of the other shapes in this book, like the Stuffed Stockings (page 42), feel free to give them a try.

Dishes for sprinkles: Pour sprinkles into a small dish so you can pinch a few to sprinkle on each pop. Pouring them from the container can result in too much waste.

Dish towels: Always have a dish towel handy. If you need to wipe off any excess

coating with your fingertips, it's better to wipe them on a dry dish towel than to risk getting water in your coating.

Double boiler: Great for larger jobs, a double boiler can heat candy coating slowly, without letting the coating get too hot, but it is not a necessity.

Lollipop sticks: Paper lollipop sticks are available in several different sizes and widths. I find the 6-in (15-cm) length to be the most versatile for displaying.

Microwave: I couldn't live without mine. You can melt candy coating colors as you need them if you have a microwave on hand.

Microwave-safe bowls: Durable plastic bowls (not melamine) are ideal for melting candy coating in the microwave. They are lightweight and can be held while dipping without burning your hands. Look for bowls that are narrow and deep. Small bowls like this will make dipping much easier and will allow you to work with less coating at a time. Wide bowls will require you to melt more coating to make it deep enough to dip. If the coating starts to get too low in the bowl to dip properly, you can transfer the coating to a coffee mug or smaller microwave-safe container. This will help you get the most out of your candy coating.

Mixer: You'll need one to have of these on hand, unless you use a store-bought cake and frosting.

Mixing bowls and spoons: Large mixing bowls and metal spoons are used to mix the cake and frosting together.

Squeeze bottles: Perfect for drizzling and decorating, squeeze bottles come in small, medium, and large sizes to meet every need. You can also pour melted candy coating into resealable plastic bags. Just snip the corner off of the bag and squeeze the coating through the hole.

Styrofoam block: Use a block that's at least 2 in (5 cm) thick, so the cake pop sticks can be inserted into it far enough that the pops won't fall over. Poke holes about 2 in (5 cm) apart in the top before you start dipping, so it will be ready when you need it. Keep the stick as straight as you can, and do not poke it all the way through. A 12-by-18-by-2-in (30-by-45-by-5-cm) block of Styrofoam can hold 48 pops.

Toothpicks: Always keep a small container of toothpicks within reach. You can use them to direct candy coating that may not have made its way completely around a cake pop. They're also the perfect disposable tool for creating textures on the surface of the candy coating.

Toothpicks are also extremely useful when adding decorations. Dip the end of a toothpick into melted candy coating and dot a little bit in position for small add-ons like sprinkles for eyes.

Additionally, you can use a toothpick to decorate the actual cake pop. Make noses, like the ones on the Santas on page 58, or even draw on the pop, as with the Gingerbread Houses (page 71).

Tweezers: Keep a pair on hand for use solely in the kitchen. They can be helpful when attaching small add-ons to a cake pop surface.

Warming tray: This is a great tool to have around if you make a lot of cake pops and use more than one color, but it's not a necessity.

Wax paper: Keep wax paper handy for lining baking sheets before resting cake balls on them; it allows them to be removed easily. Wax paper also comes in handy when shaping the cake balls. You can slide or roll the cake ball on the surface of the wax paper to help create a smoother surface.

SPRINKLES, CANDIES, AND MORE

There are lots of ways to decorate cake pops, but using sprinkles and candies are the most fun for me. Sprinkles come in so many shapes, sizes, and colors, it's challenging and exciting to see how many different ways they can be used to make a cake pop come to life. For example, jumbo heart sprinkles help finish off the scarves for the Polar Bears on page 49. Keep in mind that in many cases, the single-color sprinkles used in the cake pop projects are separated from a container of multicolored sprinkles.

But don't just focus on sprinkles; candies and other food items are just as fun to use. Check out the candy aisle in your drug store, grocery store, or even gas station. You'll start to see candy in a whole new way, inspiring your own cake pop creations.

On the next page, you'll find some of the most commonly used sprinkles, candies, and other add-ons featured in this book.

TIPS

- I like to buy seasonal sprinkles and keep them on hand. Keep in mind that the holidays are a great time to find specialty sprinkles that you can have a hard time finding other times of the year, like the Christmas tree sprinkles. Buy them when you see them and save them for when you need them.

- But if you don't, that's okay, too. There's always another candy or sprinkle to do the trick. And you can always pipe on the shapes. So don't stress if you can't find certain sprinkles. Get creative. You might even find an even cuter way to decorate your cake pops.

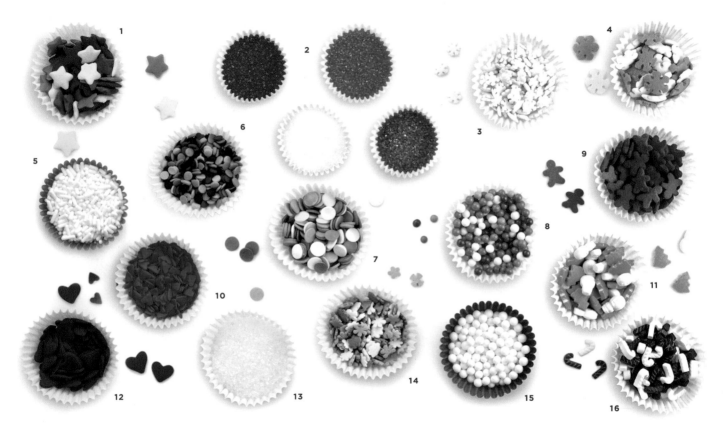

SPRINKLES

1. Jumbo stars
2. Sanding sugar
3. Snowflake sprinkles
4. Jumbo snowflakes*
5. Jimmies
6. Confetti
7. Pastel confetti
8. Mixed sugar pearls
9. Gingerbread boys*
10. Miniature hearts
11. Snowman and tree mix*
12. Jumbo hearts
13. Sugar crystals
14. Wildflower shapes
15. Sugar pearls
16. Candy canes*

*Available from Wilton.

CANDIES AND FOOD ITEMS

1. Candy necklaces
2. Pretzel sticks
3. Sixlets
4. Candy hearts
5. M&M's
6. Lemonheads
7. Mint Lifesavers
8. Starburst and Jolly Rancher Fruit Chews
9. Candy eyes
10. Small chocolate cookies
11. M&M's Minis
12. Candy snaps
13. Yogurt-covered raisins
14. Chocolate chips
15. Candy-coated sunflower seeds
16. Marshmallow bits

Displaying & Gifting

The holidays are one of my favorite times of the year to make cake pops. The season is about sharing, and that's what cake pops are all about. Make them to display in large numbers at your holiday celebration, or pack them individually in pretty wrapping to give to someone special. No matter how they are shared, you'll want them to look their best. As if they weren't cute enough already.

DISPLAYING YOUR CAKE POPS

Cake pops are showstoppers all on their own, but to showcase their cuteness, make sure you plan ahead and have a way to display them. Here are some approaches to try. From do-it-yourself displays to purchased cake pops stands, there are many ways to display your cake pops for any kind of celebration.

STYROFOAM BLOCKS: Large Styrofoam blocks are perfect to use as a stand for letting your cake pops dry. They can also be covered in scrapbook paper or gift wrap for a pretty, easy, and inexpensive display. Make holes at least 2 in (5 cm) apart to give your cake pops enough room, and remember when using a Styrofoam cake pop stand, be careful when removing the pops from the block; if all are removed from one side, the weight of the pops on

the other side are liable to tip over the Styrofoam.

GLASSWARE: Glass dishes filled with sugar make an eye-catching display for cake pops and are perfect for any holiday party. The dishes should be deep enough to keep the sticks standing upright when filled with sugar. You can also fill glass dishes with gumballs, M&M's, or even marbles for a decorative way to stabilize the cake pops. Glass candy dishes with lids are also a pretty way to display and store cake balls.

PAINTED WOOD DISPLAYS: You'll need a drill and a ruler for this one. Mark holes 2 in (5 cm) apart on a piece of wood that is about 2 in (5 cm) thick. Lighter-colored wood with less grain seems to look the best. Choose a drill bit with the same diameter as the lollipop sticks you used for your cake pops or just slightly bigger;

you want the pops to slide in and out easily. Make a mark on the drill bit about 13/4 in (4.5 cm) from the tip and stop drilling when you reach the mark; this will make sure you don't drill holes all the way through the wood.

CAKE POP STANDS: There are many fantastic premade displays available to display your cake pops. Plastic, wood, and paper cake pop stands are popping up everywhere. Round, square, or even tiered, you now have your choice of professional and beautiful bases to display your creations.

GIFTING CAKE POPS

Do you enjoy making treats to give to others? Then cake pops are the perfect choice for your holiday baking. Here are a couple of ways to present them individually or in small quantities.

BOUQUETS: Looking for a way to gift your cake pops? You can use a flowerpot, bucket, basket, or any other small cute container to display and transport them.

Place a Styrofoam ball or block inside the basket, sized to match so that it's secure, and arrange the cake pops in the Styrofoam. You can disguise the Styrofoam ball by filling in around the sticks with paper confetti, ribbon, streamers, or some other fun decoration.

GIFT TAGS, TREAT BAGS, AND RIBBON: Individual cake pops make a great impression when given as gifts. Simply wrap each cake pop individually in a small plastic treat bag, and tie with decorative ribbon or colorful twist tie. You can make them even more special by including a sweet note or gift tag. Then just hand them out at work or give them to friends.

To make tags, use a paper punch, easily available in craft stores, and punch shapes out of heavyweight card stock. Then use a regular hole punch to make two holes on either side of the shape. Add a handwritten note, and slide the tag onto the lollipop stick. Or use a computer to typeset the message you want on card stock and use a large paper punch

to punch around it. *Or you can skip all of that and visit www.bakerella.com/tags for a some downloadable holiday tag designs.*

BOXING AND SHIPPING

Most cake pops are surprisingly easy to transport or ship. For instance, the Jingle Bells (page 45) and Santas (page 58) would do fine in transit. The Sweet Soldiers (page 51), on the other hand, would be best served at home. To package your cake pops, look for pastry boxes to place them in.

Cover cake pops with treat bags and ribbon, and then lay them in alternating directions in a small pastry or cake box. Use tissue paper to fill in any gaps and to keep the pops from sliding around in the box.

- Gift them just like this or you can ship them to someone special. Tape the box shut and place it in a larger box surrounded by packing material. Then just ship overnight to ensure freshness.

Holiday Cake Pop Projects

It's time to spread some holiday cheer. In the following pages, you will find cute and festive cake pop projects to start the season off right. Make them for parties. Make them to share with friends and family. Make them just for fun. Whatever the reason, I hope you make wonderful memories and celebrate the season spreading lots of smiles along the way.

When planning a project, remember you can make your cake the night before so you can devote time the next day to dipping and decorating. It can take a few hours from start to finish, so make it even more fun—invite friends or family to help and you'll create unforgettable memories this holiday season.

Gingerheads

These happy faces with sweet confetti sprinkle cheeks are sure to bring big smiles.

YOU'LL NEED

48 uncoated cake balls (page 9)

1½-in (4-cm) round cookie cutter

48 oz (1.4 kg) chocolate or peanut butter candy coating

1 deep, microwave-safe plastic bowl

48 lollipop sticks

Styrofoam block

6 oz (170 g) white candy coating

Small, microwave-safe plastic bowl

Toothpicks

White jimmies

96 miniature pastel confetti sprinkles

96 regular pastel confetti sprinkles

TO DECORATE

1. Remove the cake balls from the refrigerator. One at a time, press them into the round cookie cutter to make nice flat, uniform shapes for the gingerbread heads. They should be about ½ in (12 mm) thick.

2. Put the shaped cakes in the freezer for about 15 minutes to firm up again for dipping. Once they are firm, transfer them to the refrigerator.

3. Melt the chocolate candy coating in the deep microwave-safe bowl, following the instructions on the package. The coating should be about 3 in (7.5 cm) deep for easier dipping.

4. When you are ready to dip, remove a few shaped cake balls at a time from the refrigerator, keeping the rest chilled.

5. One at a time, dip about ½ in (12 mm) of a lollipop stick into the melted candy coating and insert the dipped end straight into the bottom center of the circle shape pushing it no more than halfway through. Dip the cake pop into the melted coating. Gently lift the pop out of the coating and tap off any excess as described on page 22. Stand the pop firmly in a hole in the Styrofoam block. Repeat with the remaining shapes and let dry.

6. Meanwhile, melt the white candy coating in the small microwave-safe bowl to use for decorating the faces.

Continued

7. When the cake pops are completely dry, using a toothpick, dot on the melted white candy coating for glue and attach white jimmies around the perimeter of a pop, leaving a small space in between each. Use the same technique to attach 2 miniature pastel confetti sprinkles in position for the eyes. Return to the Styrofoam block. Repeat for each cake pop and let dry.

8. For the mouths, again use the toothpick and white coating to draw on a cheerful smile. While the coating is still wet, attach 2 regular pastel confetti sprinkles in position for the cheeks.

9. Let dry completely in the Styrofoam block.

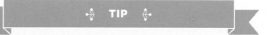

TIP

• Choose either chocolate or peanut butter candy coating for the gingerheads depending on the shade of brown you would like to achieve. You can also mix the two candy coatings. The jimmies give a clean look to these smiley cake pops, but feel free to pipe on all the white details using a squeeze bottle and white candy coating.

Welcoming Wreaths

Share these wreaths with someone new and welcome them to the world of cake pops.

YOU'LL NEED

48 uncoated cake balls (page 9)

Mini-doughnut pan

Baking sheet

48 oz (1.4 kg) dark green candy coating

Toothpicks

Deep, microwave-safe plastic bowl

48 lollipop sticks

White sugar pearls

Green sanding sugar

96 jumbo red heart candies

48 red rainbow chip sprinkles

Styrofoam block

TO DECORATE

1. Remove the cake balls from the refrigerator. Press each cake ball into the well of a mini-doughnut pan to shape it into a doughnut. Mound the top half and smooth it so you have a nice rounded doughnut, or wreath, shape. Return to the freezer for about 15 minutes to firm up.

2. After firming, use a toothpick to help retrieve the cake wreaths from the pan. Use your fingers to smooth any indentions made by the toothpick. Place the wreaths on a clean baking sheet.

3. Melt the green candy coating in the microwave-safe bowl, following the instructions on the package.

4. Using a lollipop stick, apply a layer of the melted coating to the inside ring of the wreaths and let dry. This will help create a barrier so the lollipop sticks don't push through into the center hole when you insert the stick.

5. Return the wreaths to the freezer for a few minutes to firm up again, then transfer to the refrigerator to keep firm, not frozen.

6. When you are ready to dip, remove a few cake wreaths at a time from the refrigerator, keeping the rest chilled.

7. Holding 1 wreath around the edges of its circumference with your fingertips, dunk the face horizontally into the melted candy coating. Gently lift the wreath out of the coating. While the coating is still wet, drop several white sugar pearls on top and sprinkle the surface with the sanding sugar. (Sprinkle over a bowl to catch the sugar so you can reuse it.)

Continued

8. Place the wreath, decorated-side up, on the baking sheet. Pick the spot where you will insert the lollipop stick later and make sure it is clear of coating. You can wipe off the area with your fingertip or a toothpick, if needed. The coating may fill in the center hole; just push a toothpick through the coating covering the hole while it's still wet and it will open up. Repeat with the remaining wreaths. Let dry completely.

9. Dot a small amount of the melted candy coating in position and attach 2 candy heart sprinkles and 1 rainbow chip sprinkle for the bow. Place in the freezer for a few minutes to firm up again.

10. When firm, working with 1 wreath at a time, dunk the second side in the candy coating the same way you dipped the first sides, making sure all the cake is coated. Sprinkle with the sanding sugar. Dip about ½ in (12 mm) of the lollipop stick into the melted candy coating and insert the dipped end straight into the wreath at the spot you chose earlier. Be careful not to let the stick come out the other side of the ring. Stand the pop firmly in a hole in the Styrofoam block. Repeat with the remaining wreaths.

11. Let the cake pops dry completely.

TIP

• You can also make these using the cake balls in their original round shape, or shaped into patties. First, dip in white coating, then pipe on the wreath details in green coating around the perimeter of the coated cake pop and decorate as directed above. This way is easier to dip, but the wreaths won't have an opening in the center.

Simple Snowflakes

Make snowflake shapes that pop using melted white candy coating.

YOU'LL NEED

48 uncoated cake balls (page 9)

Baking sheet

Wax paper

32 oz (910 g) white candy coating

2 deep, microwave-safe plastic bowls

Squeeze bottle

48 oz (1.4 kg) blue candy coating

48 lollipop sticks

White sanding sugar

Styrofoam block

TO DECORATE

1. Have the cake balls chilled and in the refrigerator.

2. Make snowflakes in advance. Line a baking sheet with wax paper. Melt white candy coating in one of the microwave-safe bowls, following the instructions on the package. Fill the squeeze bottle with melted coating and pipe snowflakes about 1 ½ in (3.8 cm) in diameter onto the wax paper. You can print out a snowflake template at www.bakerella.com/ tags to place under the wax paper to use as a guide. You will need 48 flakes, plus a few for breakage. Place the sheet of piped snowflakes in the freezer for a few minutes to set, then remove.

3. Melt blue candy coating in the second microwave-safe bowl, following the instructions on the package. The coating should be about 3 in (7.5 cm) deep for easier dipping.

4. When you are ready to dip, remove a few cake balls at a time from the refrigerator, keeping the rest chilled.

5. One at a time, dip about ½ in (12 mm) of the tip of a lollipop stick into the candy coating and insert the dipped end into a cake ball, pushing it no more than halfway through. Dip the cake pop into the melted coating. Lift the pop out of the coating and tap off any excess, as described on page 22.

6. Sprinkle the sanding sugar over the cake pop, covering it completely. While the coating is still wet, attach 1 piped snowflake to the front of the pop. Let the cake pops dry completely in the Styrofoam block.

Stuffed Stockings

Stuff these little stockings with sprinkles and candies for tiny toys.

YOU'LL NEED

48 uncoated cake balls (page 9) formed into stocking shapes

48 oz (1.4 kg) colored candy coating

Deep, microwave-safe plastic bowl

48 lollipop sticks

Styrofoam block

16 oz (455 g) white candy coating

Small, microwave-safe plastic bowl

Assorted sprinkles for toys, such as candy canes, gingerbread men, and flowers

Toothpicks

Sanding sugar

96 snowflake sprinkles

TO DECORATE

1. Have the shaped cake balls chilled in the refrigerator.

2. Melt the candy coating in the deep microwave-safe bowl, following the instructions on the package. The coating should be about 3 in (7.5 cm) deep for easier dipping.

3. When you are ready to dip, remove a few cake balls at a time from the refrigerator, keeping the rest chilled.

4. One at a time, dip about ½ in (12 mm) of the tip of a lollipop stick into the melted candy coating and insert the dipped end straight into the bottom of the stocking shape, pushing it no more than halfway through. Dip the cake pop into the melted coating. Gently lift the pop out of the coating and tap off any excess as described on page 22. Let dry completely in the Styrofoam block.

5. Melt white candy coating in the small microwave-safe bowl. Dip the tops into the white coating to make the cuffs. While the coating is still wet, place several of the "toy" sprinkles on top of each. Return to the Styrofoam block and let dry completely.

6. When dry, use a toothpick to apply more white candy coating on the surface of the cuffs. Sprinkle with sanding sugar over a large bowl so you can reuse it. Use the edge of a clean toothpick to straighten any edges by gently pressing it along the bottoms of the cuffs.

7. To decorate the front of the stockings, attach 2 snowflake sprinkles on each using melted candy coating as glue and dot on more coating for extra detail.

8. Let dry completely in the Styrofoam block.

Jingle Bells

Enjoy the sounds of excitement from these silver bells when you share them with others.

YOU'LL NEED

48 uncoated cake balls (page 9)

48 oz (1.4 kg) candy coating (any color)

Deep, microwave-safe plastic bowl

48 lollipop sticks

Styrofoam block

Small squeeze bottle

Edible silver spray

Paper towels

Black edible-ink pen

TO DECORATE

1. Have the cake balls chilled and in the refrigerator.

2. Melt the candy coating in the microwave-safe plastic bowl, following the instructions on the package. The coating should be about 3 in (7.5 cm) deep for easier dipping.

3. When you are ready to dip, remove a few cake balls at a time from the refrigerator, keeping the rest chilled.

4. One at a time, dip about ½ in (12 mm) of the tip of a lollipop stick into the melted candy coating and insert the dipped end straight into a cake ball, pushing it no more than halfway through. Dip the cake pop into the melted coating. Gently lift the pop out of the coating and tap off any excess as described on page 22. Stand the pop firmly in a hole in the Styrofoam block. Repeat with the remaining cake balls. Let dry completely.

5. Pour the remaining candy coating into the squeeze bottle and pipe a border around the center, or equator, of each pop. Let dry.

6. When dry, one at a time, spray the cake pops with edible silver spray to cover completely. Wrap a paper towel around the stick while you spray to make sure it stays clean. Return to the Styrofoam block and let dry.

7. When completely dry, draw 2 perpendicular lines across the top half of the pop, like a big curved X beginning and ending just above the ridge you made at the equator. Using the edible-ink pen, draw a circle at the end of each line to create the jingle bell look. You can also pipe the design on with melted black candy coating.

8. Let the cake pops dry completely in the Styrofoam block.

Peppermint Pops

No hard candy here. Sink your teeth into these soft, candy-covered cakes.

YOU'LL NEED

48 uncoated cake balls (page 9), formed into patties

48 oz (1.4 kg) white candy coating

Deep, microwave-safe plastic bowl

48 lollipop sticks

Styrofoam block

Light corn syrup

Small bowl

Small flat paintbrush

Red or pink sanding sugar

Toothpicks

TO DECORATE

1. Have the shaped cake balls chilled and in the refrigerator.

2. Melt the candy coating in a microwave-safe plastic bowl, following the instructions on the package. The coating should be about 3 in (7.5 cm) deep for easier dipping.

3. When you are ready to dip, remove a few shaped cake balls at a time from the refrigerator, keeping the rest chilled.

4. One at a time, dip about ½ in (12 mm) of the lollipop stick into the melted candy coating and insert the dipped end straight into the bottom of the patty shape, pushing it no more than halfway through. Dip the cake pop into the melted coating. Gently lift the pop out of the coating and tap off any excess as described on page 22. Stand the pop firmly in a hole in the Styrofoam block. Repeat with the remaining cake shapes. Let dry completely.

5. Pour about a tablespoon of corn syrup into the small bowl.

6. When the cake pops are completely dry, using the paintbrush, begin to paint a peppermint-candy pattern in corn syrup on one face of a cake patty. (Use the photo here as your guide.) Apply the corn syrup in a light coat and complete 1 section at a time: right after you finish painting each section, sprinkle it with sanding sugar until all the corn syrup is covered. (Sprinkle over a bowl so you can catch the sugar and reuse it.) Use a toothpick to nudge any sugar crystals that get out of place. Continue the design around the sides and back of the pop, if desired. Return to the Styrofoam block.

7. Repeat the process with the remaining cake pops and let dry completely in the Styrofoam block.

Polar Bears

Keep these cute little bears cuddled with cozy red scarves.

YOU'LL NEED

48 uncoated cake balls (page 9)

48 oz (1.4 kg) white candy coating

Deep, microwave-safe plastic bowl

144 white M&M's

48 lollipops sticks

Styrofoam block

48 black confetti sprinkles

Black edible-ink pen

8 oz (225 g) red candy coating

Small, microwave-safe plastic bowl

48 jumbo red heart sprinkles

Toothpicks

TO DECORATE

1. Have the cake balls chilled and in the refrigerator.

2. Melt the white candy coating in the deep microwave-safe bowl, following the instructions on the package. The coating should be about 3 in (7.5 cm) deep for easier dipping.

3. Remove the baking sheet of cake balls from the refrigerator. Dip 2 M&M's in the melted coating and attach to a cake ball in position for the ears. Then attach 1 M&M to the front of the pop for the bear's snout. Repeat until all the polar bear heads have ears and snout attached. Place in the freezer for a few minutes to firm up again, then transfer to the refrigerator to keep firm, not frozen.

4. When you are ready to dip, remove a few cake balls at a time from the refrigerator, keeping the rest chilled.

5. One at a time, dip about ½ in (12 mm) of the tip of a lollipop stick into the melted candy coating and insert the dipped end straight into the bottom of a polar bear head, pushing it no more than halfway through. Being very careful not to dislodge the ears or snout, dip the cake pop into the melted coating. Gently lift the pop out of the coating and tap off any excess as described on page 22. Stand the pop firmly in a hole in the Styrofoam block. Repeat with the remaining polar bear heads. Let dry completely.

6. When the pops are dry, use a toothpick to dot a small amount of the melted candy coating in position for the nose and attach a black confetti sprinkle. Draw on eyes and mouth with a black edible-ink pen and let dry

Continued

7. Meanwhile, melt the red candy coating in the small microwave-safe bowl.

8. When the cake pops are dry, working with 1 bear at a time, gently twist and remove the lollipop stick. Holding the bear upright by the top of the head, re-dip the bottom in the melted red candy coating to form the scarf. Then re-dip about ½ in (12 mm) of the lollipop stick in the coating and insert it back into the bottom of the cake pop. Attach a jumbo heart sprinkle to the red coating to finish off the scarf with a "knot." Return to the Styrofoam block. Repeat with the rest of your polar bears.

9. Let the cake pops dry completely.

TIPS

- For a fun North Pole feel, use a sturdy red-striped paper straw instead of a lollipop stick.

- If you can't find black confetti sprinkles, don't worry. You can also use the black edible-ink pen and draw on top of any other color confetti sprinkle.

Sweet Soldiers

Candy-adorned soldiers will bring anyone in the room to attention.

YOU'LL NEED

48 uncoated cake balls (page 9)

32 oz (910 g) light pink candy coating

2 deep, microwave-safe plastic bowls

Cordial cup candy mold (see page 25)

Small baking sheet

48 oz (1.4 kg) white candy coating

1 to 2 oz (30 to 55 g) chocolate candy coating

2 to 3 oz (55 to 85 g) dark pink candy coating

48 lollipop sticks

Styrofoam block

384 blue candy necklace pieces

Toothpicks

96 black candy-coated sunflower seeds

48 pink candy-coated sunflower seeds

96 pink confetti sprinkles

96 candy eyes

Black edible-ink pen

48 white confetti sprinkles

48 yogurt-covered raisins

48 jumbo snowflake sprinkles

TO DECORATE

1. Have the cake balls chilled and in the refrigerator.

2. Make the soldiers' hats in advance: Melt the light pink candy coating in one of the microwave-safe bowls, following the instructions on the package. Pour the melted coating into the cordial cup candy mold. Place in the freezer for a few minutes to set. Repeat to make a total of 48 hats. Arrange on a small baking sheet until ready to use.

3. Melt the white, chocolate, and dark pink candy coatings together in the second microwave-safe bowl, following the instructions on the package. Add more or less of each color to achieve a darker or lighter shade for the soldier heads. The coating should be about 3 in (7.5 cm) deep for easier dipping.

4. When you are ready to dip, remove a few cake balls at a time from the refrigerator, keeping the rest chilled.

Continued

5. One at a time, dip about ½ in (12 mm) of the tip of a lollipop stick into the melted candy coating and insert the dipped end straight into a cake ball, pushing it no more than halfway through. Dip the cake pop into the melted coating. Gently lift the pop out of the coating and tap off any excess, as described on page 22. Attach a pink hat on top of the cake ball and the place firmly in a hole in the Styrofoam block. Repeat with the remaining cake balls. Let dry completely.

6. Using the melted candy coating as glue, attach 8 blue candy necklace pieces around each soldier's head (4 on each side, see photo). Fill in the openings of the candies using a toothpick and the tinted white coating if you don't want to see through the candies. Return to the Styrofoam block and let dry.

7. Using a clean toothpick, and working with 1 cake pop at a time, apply small dots of the melted coating to a soldier's face in position for the mustache and attach 2 black candy-coated sunflower seeds. Dot the coating in position for the nose and attach 1 pink candy-coated sunflower seed. Using the same technique, attach 2 pink confetti sprinkles for cheeks and 2 candy eyes. Using the edible-ink pen, draw lines for teeth on a white confetti sprinkle and then attach in position for the mouth. Dot on more coating in position for the beard and attach a yogurt-covered raisin. Draw on eyebrows with the edible-ink pen. Repeat to assemble the remaining soldiers. Top off the hats with a jumbo snowflake sprinkle using melted candy coating to attach it like glue.

8. Let the cake pops dry completely in the Styrofoam block.

TO: Eva

TO: Mady

TO: Sophia

TO: Cade

Pretty Presents

Have people guess what flavor is inside these little gifts.

YOU'LL NEED

48 uncoated cake balls (page 9)

Wax paper

Baking sheet

Cookie cutter with a straight edge

48 oz (1.4 kg) white candy coating

Deep, microwave-safe plastic bowl

48 lollipop sticks

96 red candy hearts

48 red mini M&M's

Styrofoam block

Red colored cocoa butter

Small dish

Small paintbrush

TO DECORATE

1. Remove the cake balls from the refrigerator and shape them, one at a time, into small squares to form the shape of a box. You can use wax paper to aid in shaping the sides. Take each side of your cake ball and slide it on a wax paper–covered baking sheet. Rotate and repeat for each side to help create a flat surface. In addition, you can use the flat side of a metal cutter to cut off any rounded excess and to help form straight edges.

2. After shaping, put the shaped cakes in the freezer for about 15 minutes to firm up again for dipping. Once they are firm, transfer them to the refrigerator. Remove a few at a time for dipping, keeping the rest chilled.

3. Melt the candy coating in a microwave-safe plastic bowl, following the instructions on the package. The coating should be about 3 in (7.5 cm) deep for easier dipping.

4. One at a time, dip about ½ in (12 mm) of the lollipop stick into the melted candy coating and insert the stick straight into the bottom of the box shape, pushing it no more than halfway through. Dip the cake pop into the melted coating, and tap off any excess as described on page 22.

5. While the coating is wet, place two candy heart sprinkles on their sides, with pointed ends facing each other on top of the pop. Leave room to place a mini M&M's candy in between. Tilt the hearts up to form the shape of a bow before the coating sets. Let dry completely in a Styrofoam block.

6. Heat the red cocoa butter in the microwave following the directions on the bottle. Pour a little into a small dish. Paint ribbons on sides and tops of the cake pop with a brush.

7. Let the pops dry in the Styrofoam block.

Red-Nosed Reindeer

Mini pretzels for antlers and red candies for noses are perfect for everyone's favorite reindeer.

YOU'LL NEED

48 uncoated cake balls (page 9)

48 oz (1.4 kg) chocolate candy coating

Deep, microwave-safe plastic bowl

48 lollipop sticks

Styrofoam block

96 miniature alphabet-shaped pretzels or mini pretzel twists

Toothpicks

48 red peanut M&M's or red Lemonheads

96 miniature white confetti sprinkles

Black edible-ink pen

TO DECORATE

1. Have the cake balls chilled and in the refrigerator.

2. Melt the chocolate candy coating in the microwave-safe bowl, following the instructions on the package. The coating should be about 3 in (7.5 cm) deep for easier dipping.

3. When you are ready to dip, remove a few cake balls at a time from the refrigerator, keeping the rest chilled.

4. One at a time, dip about ½ in (12 mm) of the tip of a lollipop stick into the melted candy coating and insert the dipped end straight into a cake ball, pushing it no more than halfway through. Dip the cake pop into the melted coating. Gently lift the pop out of the coating and tap off any excess, as described on page 22. Immediately attach 1 pretzel on each side of the reindeer head for antlers. Hold them in place until the candy coating sets like glue. Stand the pop firmly in a hole in the Styrofoam block. Repeat with the remaining cake balls. Let the pops dry completely.

5. Using a toothpick, dot a small amount of the melted candy coating in position for the nose and attach 1 red candy. Hold the nose in place until the coating sets. Use a clean toothpick to dot a small amount of coating in position for the eyes and attach 2 white miniature confetti sprinkles. Return to the Styrofoam block. Repeat with the rest of your reindeer. Using the edible-ink pen, draw on mouths and dot the eyes.

6. Let the cake pops dry completely.

Santas

These jolly fellas bring good cheer and hearty ho-ho-hos.

YOU'LL NEED

48 uncoated cake balls (page 9)

3 deep, microwave-safe plastic bowls

64 oz (1.8 kg) white candy coating

2 to 3 oz (55 to 85 g) pink candy coating

1 to 2 oz (30 to 55 g) chocolate candy coating

48 lollipop sticks

Styrofoam block

16 oz (455 g) red candy coating

Toothpicks

48 white Sixlets

48 pink confetti sprinkles

96 white candy-coated sunflower seeds

Sanding sugar

Black edible-ink pen

Peach edible-ink pen

TO DECORATE

1. Have the cake balls chilled and in the refrigerator.

2. In one of the microwave-safe bowls, melt together 48 oz (1.4 kg) of the white candy coating with the pink and chocolate candy coating, following the instructions on the package. Add more or less of each color to achieve a darker or lighter shade for Santa's face. The coating should be about 3 in (7.5 cm) deep for easier dipping.

3. When you are ready to dip, remove a few cake balls at a time from the refrigerator, keeping the rest chilled.

4. One at a time, dip about ½ in (12 mm) of the tip of a lollipop stick into the melted candy coating and insert the dipped end straight into a cake ball, pushing it no more than halfway through. Dip the cake pop into the melted coating. Gently lift the pop out of the coating and tap off any excess as described on page 22. Stand the pop firmly in a hole in the Styrofoam block. Repeat with the remaining cake balls. Let dry.

5. Meanwhile, melt the red candy coating in a microwave-safe bowl. When dry, dip each pop in the red coating about one-third of the way up the sides, at a slight angle. Return to the Styrofoam block and let dry completely.

Continued

6. Melt the remaining white candy coating in another microwave-safe bowl. Using a toothpick, dot some of the melted white coating on one side of each cake pop in position for the ball of Santa's hat, and attach a white Sixlet to each.

7. Using the toothpick, apply more white coating for each Santa's beard. Place a pink confetti sprinkle for a mouth on each. Continue layering white coating on the pop for a nice full beard. Once it starts to set, it's easy to continue adding layers. Let dry completely in the Styrofoam block.

8. Dot on more melted white coating above the confetti sprinkles and attach 2 white sunflower seeds to each in position for the mustache and let dry.

9. Apply more white coating at the base of the hat and sprinkle sanding sugar on top while the coating is still wet. (Sprinkle over a bowl so you can catch the sugar and reuse it.) Use some of the remaining tinted white coating to dot on a cute nose using a toothpick. Using the black edible-ink pen, draw eyes on the Santas. Draw cheeks with the peach edible-ink pen. Dab the cheeks so they look blended.

10. Return each Santa to the Styrofoam block as you finish. Let the cake pops dry completely.

Freckled Elves

Tinker in the kitchen and create a workshop full of Santa's sweet little helpers.

YOU'LL NEED

48 uncoated cake balls (page 9) formed into oval shapes

48 oz (1.4 kg) white candy coating

Deep, microwave-safe plastic bowl

2 to 3 oz (55 to 85 g) pink candy coating

1 to 2 oz (30 to 55 g) chocolate candy coating

48 lollipop sticks

Styrofoam block

16 oz (455 g) red candy coating

2 small microwave-safe plastic bowls

Toothpicks

16 oz (455 g) green candy coating

Black edible-ink pen

Pink edible-ink pen

Sanding sugar

48 white candy necklace pieces

TO DECORATE

1. Have the oval-shaped cake balls chilled and in the refrigerator.

2. Melt the white candy coating following the instructions on the package. The coating should be about 3 in (7.5 cm) deep for easier dipping. Reserve some of the plain white candy coating in a small bowl to use for the hats; set aside. Tint the remaining white coating with the pink and chocolate, melting as before to mix. Add more or less of each color to achieve a darker or lighter shade for the elf head.

3. When you are ready to dip, remove a few oval-shaped cake balls at a time from the refrigerator, keeping the rest chilled.

4. One at a time, dip about ½ in (12 mm) of the tip of a lollipop stick into the melted candy coating and insert the dipped end straight into the bottom of the cake ball, pushing it no more than halfway through. Dip the cake pop into the melted coating. Gently lift the pop out of the coating and tap off any excess as described on page 22. Stand the pop firmly in a hole in the Styrofoam block. Repeat with the remaining oval shapes. Let dry completely.

Continued

5. Meanwhile, melt the red candy coating in one of the small microwave-safe bowls. When the pops are dry, using a toothpick, draw the outline of the bangs on the foreheads of the elves with the red coating. Fill in the area with more red coating and let dry. You only need to coat the area that will show in front of the hat. Return to the Styrofoam block and let dry.

6. Melt the green candy coating in the second small microwave-safe bowl. When dry, dip each cake pop elf in at an angle to form the hat, leaving the bangs showing. (You can let the green coating set for a few minutes to thicken before you dip. Then if you hold the pop upside down for a few seconds, it will form a subtle pointed hat.) Let dry.

7. Using a clean toothpick, dot a small amount of the tinted white coating to form a nose and ears for each elf and let dry.

8. Use the edible-ink pen to draw on eyes and a mouth. Let dry. Use a pink or peach edible ink pen to draw freckles or blend on the pops for rosy cheeks.

9. Using another clean toothpick, draw along of the edge of the hat with the reserved melted white candy coating. While still wet, sprinkle sanding sugar on top and let dry. (Sprinkle over a bowl so you can catch the sugar and reuse it.) Dot a little tinted white coating at the bottom of each elf head and attach a candy necklace piece on the lollipop stick for a collar.

10. Let the cake pops dry completely in the Styrofoam block.

Bright Lights

These Christmas light cake pops will brighten up any room with sweetness.

YOU'LL NEED

48 uncoated cake balls (page 9), formed into rounded cone shapes

Small bowl

Small paintbrush

Silver luster dust

Clear extract like almond, lemon, or vanilla

96 mint Life Savers

Small baking sheet

48 oz (1.4 kg) red, green, blue, or yellow candy coating

Deep, microwave-safe plastic bowl

48 lollipop sticks

Styrofoam block

TO DECORATE

1. Have the shaped cake balls chilled and in the refrigerator.

2. Make the Life Saver "threads" for the light bulbs in advance: In a small bowl, using a paintbrush, mix a small amount of luster dust with a few drops of extract. Stack 2 of the Life Savers together and paint on the luster mixture. The mints will sticks together when the liquid dries. Repeat to make 48 stacks. Set aside the stacks on a small baking sheet as you finish them.

3. Melt the candy coating in the microwave-safe bowl, following the instructions on the package. The coating should be about 3 in (7.5 cm) deep for easier dipping.

4. When you are ready to dip, remove a few cone-shaped cake balls at a time from the refrigerator, keeping the rest chilled.

5. One at a time, dip about ½ in (12 mm) of the tip of a lollipop stick into the melted candy coating, and insert the dipped end straight into the bottom of a shaped cone, pushing it no more than halfway through. Dip the cake pop into the melted coating. Gently lift the pop out of the coating and tap off any excess, as described on page 22. Immediately slide a stacked pair of silver-painted Life Savers onto the lollipop stick while the candy coating is still wet so the mints will attach to the pop. Hold it in place until the coating sets like glue. Stand the pop firmly in a hole in the Styrofoam block. Repeat to assemble the remaining light bulbs.

6. Alternatively, you can dip all the pops first and then glue the mints to the pops using the melted candy coating.

7. Let the pops dry completely in the Styrofoam block.

Ornaments

You can pipe designs or use sprinkles on these sugary spheres.

YOU'LL NEED

48 uncoated cake balls (page 9)

48 oz (1.4 kg) candy coating, any color

Deep, microwave-safe plastic bowl

48 lollipop sticks

Styrofoam block

Toothpicks

White sugar crystals

48 white candy necklace pieces

Confetti sprinkles

Silver luster dust

Clear extract

Small paintbrush

TO DECORATE

1. Have the cake balls chilled and in the refrigerator.

2. Melt the candy coating in the microwave-safe plastic bowl, following the instructions on the package. The coating should be about 3 in (7.5 cm) deep for easier dipping.

3. When you are ready to dip, remove a few cake balls at a time from the refrigerator, keeping the rest chilled.

4. One at a time, dip about ½ in (12 mm) of the tip of a lollipop stick into the melted candy coating and insert the dipped end straight into a cake ball, pushing it no more than halfway through. Dip the cake pop into the melted coating deep enough that it coats some of the stick as well. Gently lift the pop out of the coating and tap off any excess as described on page 22. Place in a Styrofoam block to dry.

5. Use a toothpick dipped in coating to draw lines around each pop. While the drawn coating is wet, sprinkle with white sugar crystals to coat. Return to the Styrofoam block and let dry.

6. When dry, place dots of melted coating around the center of the cake pop and attach confetti sprinkles.

7. When completely dry, slide one candy necklace piece on each lollipop stick and twist gently to create a clean straight edge where the candy piece and the candy coating meet. To attach candy piece, dot a little melted coating on the stick, place candy in position, and let dry.

8. To finish, combine silver luster dust with a small amount of clear extract to create a liquid and paint each candy necklace piece silver with a small paintbrush.

9. Let the cake pops dry completely in the Styrofoam block. Display with sticks up in a dish of sugar or candy.

Cheery Christmas Trees

All you need is a toothpick to create branches for these cheerful trees.

YOU'LL NEED

48 uncoated cake balls (page 9) formed into cone shapes with a flat bottom

48 oz (1.4 kg) white candy coating

Deep, microwave-safe plastic bowl

48 lollipop sticks

48 jumbo yellow star sprinkles

Styrofoam block

Toothpicks

Yellow sanding sugar

Multicolored sugar pearls

Candies like Starburst or Jolly Rancher Fruit Chews

TO DECORATE

1. Have the cake cones chilled and in the refrigerator.

2. Melt the white candy coating in the microwave-safe bowl, following the instructions on the package. The coating should be about 3 in (7.5 cm) deep for easier dipping.

3. When you are ready to dip, remove a few cake cones at a time from the refrigerator, keeping the rest chilled.

4. One at a time, dip about ½ in (12 mm) of the tip of a lollipop stick into the melted candy coating and insert the dipped end straight into the flat bottom of a cake cone, pushing it no more than halfway through. Dip the cake pop into the melted candy coating. Gently lift the pop out of the coating and tap off any excess as described on page 22. While the coating is still wet, attach a yellow jumbo star sprinkle on top and let dry in a Styrofoam block.

5. When dry, use a toothpick dipped in the melted white coating to texturize the trees. Start at the bottom and apply coating in short strokes, pulling towards the top. Continue around the pop as you work toward the top. Overlapping strokes will help create a seamless look. The strokes will hold their shape better if the coating has started to thicken and set. Let trees dry in a Styrofoam block.

Continued

6. When dry, use a toothpick to draw coating in a spiral around the pop for garland. While the coating is wet, sprinkle yellow sanding sugar over trees above a small bowl so you can reuse any sanding sugar that doesn't stick to the tree. Repeat with remaining pops and let dry. For decorations, dot on white candy coating around the tree and attach multicolor sugar pearls for ornaments.

7. Make your trees even cuter by adding candy presents. Dot coating on the bottom of the tree and hold candies in place until the coating sets and they are attached like glue. Just make sure to unwrap your presents before you eat the cake pops.

Gingerbread Houses

These tiny snow-coated and candy-covered houses will fill your heart with happiness.

YOU'LL NEED

48 uncoated cake balls (page 9)

Wax paper

Baking sheet

Cookie cutter with straight edge

48 oz (1.4 kg) chocolate or peanut butter candy coating

Deep, microwave-safe plastic bowl

48 lollipop sticks

Styrofoam block

16 oz (455 g) white candy coating

Small, microwave-safe plastic bowl

Toothpicks

Miniature confetti sprinkles or sanding sugar

Assorted sprinkles like candy canes, gingerbread men, regular and mini confetti, snowflakes, trees, flowers, and mini marshmallow bits for decoration

Red edible-ink pen

TO DECORATE

1. Remove the baking sheet of cake balls from the refrigerator. Shape them, one at a time, into squares with a gabled top—that is, tiny houses. You can use wax paper to aid in shaping the sides: take a cake ball and slide each side on a wax paper-covered baking sheet to create a flat surface. Rotate and repeat for each side to help create a flat surface. Lay the house on its back and use the flat side of a metal cutter to cut off any rounded excess and form a sharp pointed roof. Shape all the cake balls, return to the baking sheet, and place in the freezer for about 15 minutes to firm up, then transfer to the refrigerator to keep firm, not frozen.

2. Melt the chocolate candy coating in the deep microwave-safe bowl, following the instructions on the package. The coating should be about 3 in (7.5 cm) deep for easier dipping.

3. When you are ready to dip, remove a few house-shaped cake balls at a time from the refrigerator, keeping the rest chilled.

Continued

4. One at a time, dip about ½ in (12 mm) of the tip of a lollipop stick into the melted candy coating and insert the stick straight into the bottom of a shaped cake ball, pushing it no more than halfway through. Dip the cake pop into the melted coating. Gently lift the pop out of the coating and tap off any excess as described on page 22. Stand the pop firmly in a hole in the Styrofoam block. Repeat with the remaining house shapes. Let the pops dry in the Styrofoam block.

5. Meanwhile, melt the white candy coating in the small microwave-safe bowl. You can apply the coating in a variety of ways to decorate the houses.

6. Use a toothpick to apply coating to the roof. While the coating is still wet, attach miniature confetti sprinkles to the top for shingles or sprinkle on sanding sugar for snow. (Sprinkle over a bowl to catch the sugar so you can reuse it.)

7. You can also outline the edges of the houses and add snow to the bottom by drawing on the pop with a toothpick dipped into the white coating. Attach assorted sprinkles like trees and gingerbread men to the front of the pop using the candy coating as glue. You can also accent the sprinkles with candy coating by adding snow to the trees or faces to the gingerbread men using a toothpick.

8. Draw a peppermint design on white confetti sprinkles using the edible-ink pen.

9. As each house is finished, place it in the Styrofoam block. Let the cake pops dry completely.

• You can decorate these as much or as little as you like. Simply outlining the edges and coating the roof will still create cute little houses.

Delightful Dreidels

Cut lollipop sticks are a fun way to put a spin on these pops.

YOU'LL NEED

48 uncoated cake balls (page 9), formed into squares

48 oz (1.4 kg) white candy coating

Deep, microwave-safe plastic bowl

48 Hershey's Kisses

48 lollipop sticks

Styrofoam block

Toothpicks

White and/or blue sugar crystals

Scissors

TO DECORATE

1. Have the square-shaped cake balls chilled in the refrigerator.

2. Melt the white candy coating in a microwave-safe plastic bowl, following the instructions on the package. The coating should be about 3 in (7.5 cm) deep for easier dipping.

3. Remove the shaped squares from the refrigerator. Dip the bottom of a Hershey's Kiss candy into the melted candy coating and attach it to the top side of a square. Repeat with the remaining kisses and cake shapes. Return to the refrigerator and let dry completely.

4. When you are ready to dip, remove a few Kisses-topped cake squares at a time from the refrigerator, keeping the rest chilled.

5. One at a time, dip about ½ in (12 mm) of the tip of a lollipop stick into the melted white candy coating and insert the dipped end straight into the bottom of a square-shaped cake ball, pushing it no more than halfway through. Dip the entire cake pop with candy attached into the melted coating. Gently lift the pop out of the coating and tap off any excess, as described on page 22. Stand the pop firmly in a hole in the Styrofoam block. Repeat for remaining dreidels. Let dry completely.

6. When dry, use a toothpick dipped in the melted candy coating to coat all the edges of the pop and toward the pointed end of the dreidel. Sprinkle white or blue sugar crystals on the lines of candy coating until covered completely. (Sprinkle over a bowl to catch the sugar so you can reuse it.) Return to the Styrofoam block. Repeat with the remaining dreidels.

7. Let the cake pops dry completely. When dry, use the scissors to trim lollipop sticks about 1 in (2.5 cm) long, to resemble the short handles of traditional dreidels.

Colorful Cardinals

Use pretzels for branches and these cake pops will stick out at any holiday party.

YOU'LL NEED

48 uncoated cake balls (page 9)

Wax paper

Baking sheet

48 oz (1.4 kg) red candy coating

Deep, microwave-safe plastic bowl

48 lollipop sticks

Styrofoam block

Small microwave-safe plastic bowl

Small amount of white candy coating

Black edible-ink pen

Toothpicks

48 orange rainbow chip sprinkles

96 red jumbo heart sprinkles

48 pretzel sticks

96 orange wildflower sprinkles

96 Christmas tree sprinkles

TO DECORATE

1. Remove chilled cake balls from the refrigerator. Shape them, one at a time, into a rounded crescent moon shape. You can use wax paper to aid in shaping: take a cake ball and roll it on a wax paper–covered baking sheet. Gently roll back and forth, pushing from the middle to lengthen and create symmetrical pointed ends. Use gentle pressure to create a smooth, rounded surface. Bend into a crescent and return to the baking sheet.

2. Put the shaped cakes in the freezer for about 15 minutes to firm up again, then transfer them to the refrigerator to keep firm, not frozen.

3. Melt the red candy coating in the deep microwave-safe bowl, following the instructions on the package. The coating should be about 3 in (7.5 cm) deep for easier dipping.

4. When you are ready to dip, remove a few cake balls at a time from the refrigerator, keeping the rest chilled.

5. One at a time, dip about ½ in (12 mm) of the tip of a lollipop stick into the melted candy coating and then insert the dipped end straight into the bottom, or belly, of the cardinal shape, pushing it no more than halfway through. One end should be pointed up and forward (the head) and the other is pointed down and back (the tail).

Continued

Dip the cake pop into the melted coating. Gently lift the pop out of the coating and tap off any excess as described on page 22. Stand the pop firmly in a hole in the Styrofoam block. Repeat with the remaining cake balls. Let the pops dry completely in the Styrofoam block.

6. Meanwhile, in the small microwave-safe bowl, melt the white candy coating.

7. When the pops are dry, using the edible-ink pen, draw on a rounded heart shape on each pop for the cardinal's face. Using a toothpick, dot the eyes on each face with the melted white candy coating. Using the toothpick, dot the white coating in position for the beaks and attach 1 orange rainbow chip sprinkle on each.

8. Use the toothpick again, dot on red candy coating in position for the wings and attach a jumbo heart sprinkle "wing" on either side of the cardinal bodies. Dot more coating on the front of the cake pops where the lollipop stick is inserted and attach a pretzel stick on each for a tree branch, as if the cardinal was perching. Return the pops to the Styrofoam block as you work and let dry completely.

9. When dry, dot on more red coating on the bottom of the cardinal bodies where the pretzel sticks are attached and place 2 orange wildflower sprinkles in position for feet. Use the same technique to attach 2 Christmas tree sprinkles on each pretzel stick for leaves. Let dry in the Styrofoam block. When dry, use a clean toothpick to dot 3 small berries on the leaves using the red candy coating.

10. Let the cake pops dry completely.

→ TIPS ←

- You can also add a small amount of white candy coating on the branches for snow.

- If you choose not to add branches, just attach the feet to the bottom front of the cardinal body.

- You can also make your own leaves by piping green candy coating on wax paper. Let dry and they are ready to use.

Frosty Friends

Warm someone's heart with these cheerful treats.

YOU'LL NEED

48 uncoated cake balls (page 9)

48 oz (1.4 kg) white candy coating

2 deep, microwave-safe plastic bowls

24 lollipop sticks

24 orange candy-coated sunflower seeds

Styrofoam block

Toothpicks

72 miniature confetti sprinkles

Black edible-ink pen

5 oz (140 g) blue candy coating

Sanding sugar

Licorice Belts (cut into 12 2-inch strips)

24 green M&M's Minis

12 one-inch chocolate cookies

12 large dark chocolate chips, such as Ghirardelli

TO DECORATE

1. Half of the balls should be rolled about 1.5 in (4 cm) in diameter for the bodies and the other half about 1.25 in (3 cm) in diameter for the heads.

2. Have the cake balls chilled and in the refrigerator.

3. Melt the white candy coating in a microwave-safe bowl, following the instructions on the package. The coating should be about 3 in (7.5 cm) deep for easier dipping.

4. When you are ready to dip, remove two cake balls at a time (one large and one small) from the refrigerator, keeping the rest chilled.

5. One at a time, dip about ½ in (12 mm) of the tip of a lollipop stick into the melted candy coating and insert the dipped end straight through the bottom of the larger ball and half-way into the smaller cake ball placed on top. Dip the stacked cake pop into the melted coating. Gently lift the pop out of the coating and tap off any excess, as described on page 22.

6. While the coating is still wet, attach a sunflower seed in position for the nose. Stand the pop firmly in a hole in the Styrofoam block. Let dry completely.

7. When dry, use a toothpick to dot a small amount of the melted white candy coating in position for buttons and attach 3 confetti sprinkles to the belly of each snowman. Draw eyes and a dotted smile on each head with the edible-ink pen. Return to the Styrofoam block and let dry completely.

Continued

8. For scarves: Melt blue candy coating following the directions on the package. Use a toothpick to apply coating around the snowman's neck, with two ends hanging down on one side. While still wet, sprinkle sanding sugar on top. Let dry and dot more coating on the top of the scarf for a knot. Sprinkle sanding sugar again to cover. Sprinkle sugar over a large bowl to catch and reuse.

9. For earmuffs: Attach cut strips of licorice belt candies across the heads of half of the snowmen with a little melted white candy coating as glue. Then dot more candy coating on the cake pop at either end of the licorice belt and attach one M&M Minis (M-side down) on each side.

10. For hats: Dot a small amount of white coating on the a snowman head and attach 1 chocolate cookie. Then dot melted blue candy coating into the center of the cookie. Using even pressure and keeping the chip and cookie flat, push 1 chocolate chip, pointed-side down, into the blue coating. As you push, the melted candy coating will move up the sides of the chip, giving you a blue ribbon for the hat. Sprinkle with sanding sugar and return to the Styrofoam block.

11. Repeat to finish all the snowmen and let the cake pops dry completely.

- You can use small snack-size chocolate cookies like Keebler Dark Chocolate Right Bites or Murray Sugar Free Bites for the hat bases. And try Rainbow Airheads Xtremes Sour Belts or Rips Licorice Belts if making earmuffs. Use a pair of kitchen scissors to cut them to the size you need.

Jolly Holly

Simple and festive, these cake pops inspired by my friend Marian of Sweetopia.net are berry sweet.

YOU'LL NEED

48 uncoated cake balls (page 9)

48 oz (1.4 kg) chocolate candy coating

2 deep, microwave-safe plastic bowls

48 lollipop sticks

Styrofoam block

16 oz (455 g) white candy coating

Squeeze bottle

96 Christmas tree sprinkles

Red candy writer or a small amount of red candy coating

144 red sugar pearls

TO DECORATE

1. Have the cake balls chilled and in the refrigerator.

2. Melt the chocolate candy coating in a microwave-safe plastic bowl, following the instructions on the package. The coating should be about 3 in (7.5 cm) deep for easier dipping.

3. When you are ready to dip, remove a few cake balls at a time from the refrigerator, keeping the rest chilled.

4. One at a time, dip about ½ in (12 mm) of the lollipop stick into the melted candy coating and insert the stick straight into the bottom of the cake ball, pushing it no more than halfway through. Dip the cake pop into the melted coating, and tap off any excess as described on page 22.

5. Place in the Styrofoam block to dry.

6. Melt the white candy coating in a microwave-safe plastic bowl, following the instructions on the package. Pour melted candy coating into a squeeze bottle and pipe coating on top of cake pop in a wavy design so it appears to be dripping down the side. You can also use a toothpick dipped in coating to apply it to the pop if it's easier for you.

7. Place 2 Christmas tree sprinkles into the coating while it is still wet. Tilt the pointed ends of the tree upward slightly and let dry.

8. Using a red candy writer or melted red candy coating, place 3 dots of coating on the surface of the tree sprinkles and attach 3 red sugar pearls for berries.

9. Let dry completely in a Styrofoam block.

Festive Pets

Dress up these pet pops with reindeer antlers for some holiday fun.

YOU'LL NEED

48 uncoated cake balls (page 9)

48 oz (1.4 kg) white candy coating

3 deep, microwave-safe plastic bowls

48 white jumbo heart sprinkles

48 lollipop sticks

Toothpicks

24 pink rainbow chip sprinkles

Black edible-ink pen

4 oz (110 g) chocolate candy coating

48 chocolate chips

24 brown rainbow chip sprinkles

48 candy necklace pieces

Small amount of green candy coating

96 gingerbread sprinkles

Styrofoam block

TO DECORATE

1. Have the cake balls chilled and in the refrigerator.

2. For the cats, melt white candy coating in a deep microwave-safe plastic bowl, following the instructions on the package.

The coating should be about 3 in (7.5 cm) deep for easier dipping.

3. Dip 2 white jumbo heart sprinkles in the melted coating and attach to the pop in position for ears. Repeat until all the cats have ears attached. Place in the freezer for a few minutes to firm up again, then transfer to the refrigerator to keep firm, not frozen.

4. One at a time, dip about ½ in (12 mm) of the tip of a lollipop stick into the melted candy coating, and insert the stick straight into the bottom of a cake ball, pushing it no more than halfway through. Dip the entire cake pop with ears attached into the melted coating. Gently lift the pop out of the coating and tap off any excess as described on page 22. Place in a Styrofoam block to dry. Repeat with half of the cake balls. Let the pops dry completely.

5. When dry, use a toothpick to dot a small amount of melted candy coating in position for the nose and attach a pink rainbow chip sprinkle. Draw on eyes and a mouth with the edible-ink pen and let dry.

Continued

6. Melt the chocolate coating in a second microwave-safe plastic bowl. Then combine some of the chocolate with the remaining white candy coating to create a light brown color for the dogs and the stripes for the cats. Add more or less chocolate to achieve a darker or lighter shade. Make sure to reserve a little white candy coating to use for details at the end.

7. Use a toothpick dipped in the light brown coating to draw stripes on the cats forehead and cheeks and let dry.

8. Then with the remaining cake balls, dip them in the light brown coating. Attach two chocolate chips on the top in position for ears and let dry completely.

9. Draw eyes and mouth with a black edible ink pen. When dry, use a toothpick dipped in brown coating to create snouts for the dogs. While the coating is still wet, place a brown rainbow chip sprinkle in position for the nose and let dry.

10. With reserved white melted candy coating, dot on details for all the eyes with a toothpick and draw spots on some of the dogs for extra detail. You can also dot some coating on the bottom of the cake pop and slide a candy necklace piece on the stick to attach to the pop for collars.

11. When dry, melt green candy coating in a third microwave-safe bowl. Use a toothpick dipped in coating to draw a headband on the top of each pet. While the coating is still wet, attach two gingerbread sprinkles onto the headband upside down for reindeer antlers. Hold in place until the antlers set.

12. Let dry completely in the Styrofoam block.

Snow Globes

There's a flurry of cake pop possibilities. This cute design was inspired by Nadia Pereira, one of the Pop Stars featured on Bakerella.com.

YOU'LL NEED

48 uncoated cake balls (page 9)

32 oz (910 g) red candy coating

3 deep, microwave-safe plastic bowls

1 in (2.5 cm) candy cup chocolate mold (see page 25)

96 lollipop sticks

Small baking sheet

48 oz (1.4 kg) light blue candy coating

White nonpareils

Styrofoam block

Toothpicks

White confetti sprinkles or marshmallow bits

Small amount of white candy coating

White sanding sugar

Snowflake sprinkles

Black, orange and blue edible ink pens

TO DECORATE

1. Have the cake balls chilled and in the refrigerator.

2. Make the bases in advance. Melt the red candy coating in a microwave-safe plastic bowl following the instructions on the package and pour into the candy cup mold cavities. Place a lollipop stick in the center of each mold shape and place in the freezer for several minutes to set. Repeat until all the snow globe bases are made. Note: if the coating is too fluid when you fill the cavities the sticks will fall over. If this happens, let the coating set for a few minutes in the mold and insert the sticks before they dry completely. Let prepared bases rest on a small baking sheet.

3. Melt blue candy coating in second microwave-safe plastic bowl, following the instructions on the package. The coating should be about 3 in (7.5 cm) deep for easier dipping.

4. When you are ready to dip, remove a few cake balls at a time from the refrigerator, keeping the rest chilled.

Continued

5. One at a time, dip about ½ in (12 mm) of the lollipop stick into the melted candy coating and insert the stick straight into the bottom of the cake ball, pushing it no more than halfway through. Dip the cake pop into the melted coating, and tap off any excess as described on page 22.

6. Sprinkle pops with nonpareils for snow while the coating is still wet and place in the Styrofoam block to dry.

7. To attach globes to the bases, place a small amount of melted red candy coating on the top of each base. Remove the globe from the stick it was placed on to dry and then place it hole down on to the red candy coating covered base to attach like glue. Let dry completely.

8. When dry, dot coating on the ball in position for the snowman and attach two confetti sprinkles. You can also use marsh-mallow bits (pressed together with your fingers) for a bigger snowman body. Next, melt and apply white candy coating on the bottom of the pop using a toothpick. Sprinkle sanding sugar on while it's still wet for fallen snow. Pour sprinkles over a bowl to catch and reuse any that don't attach to the pop. Use a toothpick if necessary to clean up any edges.

9. Dot coating in several places on the top of the pop and attach snowflake sprinkles for larger flurries.

10. Draw on snowman details with the black, blue and orange edible ink pens.

11. Let dry completely in the Styrofoam block.

Visit bakerella.com/pop-stars for more fun cake pop creations from the readers of Bakerella.

Resources

CAKE- AND CANDY-MAKING *Candy coatings, lollipop sticks, treat bags, and more can be found at the following online sources.*

Cake Art:
www.cakeartpartystore.com

Candyland Crafts:
www.candylandcrafts.com

CK Products:
www.ckproducts.com

Confectionery House:
www.confectioneryhouse.com

Kitchenkrafts.com:
www.kitchenkrafts.com

CANDY *Grocery stores, drug stores, and even gas stations carry a wide assortment of candies to get your creative juices flowing. Here are a few online options as well.*

Candy Direct:
www.candydirect.com

Candy Warehouse:
www.candywarehouse.com

Dylan's Candy Bar:
www.dylanscandybar.com

M&M's:
www.mms.com
(purchase the color you want)

CANDY COATINGS *Find chocolate, vanilla, and colored candy coatings from a variety of outlets. Chocolate and vanilla varieties are also available from grocery store chains like Kroger. Shades can vary from manufacturers.*

Kroger:
www.kroger.com

Make 'n Mold:
www.makenmold.com

Merckens:
www.adm.com
(available from cake and candy suppliers and on amazon.com)

Wilton:
www.wilton.com

CANDY COLORING

Chefmaster Candy Color:
(available from cake and candy
suppliers)

Make 'n Mold:
www.makenmold.com

Wilton:
www.wilton.com

CANDY OIL

LorAnn Oils:
www.lorannoils.com

EDIBLE-INK PENS

Americolor:
www.americolorcorp.com
(available on amazon.com)

CRAFT STORES *Retail craft stores
also carry most of the basics you'll
need for many of the projects,
including treat bags, ribbon, cookie
cutters, and lollipop sticks.*

A.C. Moore:
www.acmoore.com

Hobby Lobby:
www.hobbylobby.com

Jo-Ann Fabric and Craft Stores:
www.joann.com

Michaels:
www.michaels.com

CANDY MOLDS

Cordial cups mold
www.wilton.com

1-in (2.5-cm) candy cup mold [#90-5604]
www.cakeart.com

SEASONAL SPRINKLES

Cake supply stores, craft stores,
and online:
www.amazon.com
www.wilton.com

EDIBLE SILVER SPRAY

Cake supply stores and online:
www.chefmaster.com

LUSTER DUST, PLAIN + COLORED
COCOA BUTTER

Cake supply stores and online

MARSHMALLOW BITS

www.nuts.com

MINI-DOUGHNUT PAN

www.wilton.com

STRIPED STRAWS

www.bakeitpretty.com
www.shopsweetlulu.com

Cake Pops Projects Photo Index

PAGE 35

PAGE 37

PAGE 41

PAGE 42

PAGE 45

PAGE 46

PAGE 49

PAGE 51

PAGE 55

PAGE 57

PAGE 58

CAKE POPS
HOLIDAYS by *Bakerella*

PAGE 61

PAGE 65

PAGE 67

PAGE 69

PAGE 71

PAGE 75

PAGE 77

PAGE 79

PAGE 83

PAGE 85

PAGE 87

Index

A

Add-ons, edible   24, 27–29

B

Baking sheets   25

Basic Cake Pops   9–12

Bears, Polar   49–50

Bells, Jingle   45

Bloom   14

Bouquets   31

Bowls   26

Boxing   31

Bright Lights   65

Buttercream

    Buttercream Frosting   17

    Chocolate Buttercream   17

C

Cake pans   25

Cake pops. *See also individual recipes*

    Basic Cake Pops   9–12

    boxing and shipping   31

    crumbling cake for   18

    decorating   27–29

    definition of   7

    dipping   22–23

    displaying   30–31

    equipment for   25–27, 30–31

    getting started with   7, 18

    as gifts   31

    ingredients for   23–25

    mixing base for   19

    shapes for   19–20

    stands for   31

    storing   13

    tips for   12, 19

    troubleshooting   13–14

    yields for   19

Cakes

    Chocolate Cake   16

    crumbling   18

    from mixes   15

    Red Velvet Cake   16–17

    suitable, for cake pops   23

    Yellow Cake   15

Candies, decorating with   27, 29

Candy coating

    chocolate as alternative to   13, 21–22

    colors   21, 22, 24

    dipping cake pops into   22–23

    finding   13, 23–24

    flavorings for   21, 24

    as glue   23

    melting   20–21

    storing   20

    thinning   21

    troubleshooting   13–14

    uses for   20

Candy coloring — 21, 24
Candy-flavoring oils — 21, 24
Candy gloves — 25
Candy molds — 25
Candy writers — 24
Cardinals, Colorful — 77–78
Cheery Christmas Trees — 69–70
Chocolate
    as candy coating — 13, 21–22
    Chocolate Buttercream — 17
    Chocolate Cake — 16
    Chocolate Cream Cheese Frosting — 17
Christmas Trees, Cheery — 69–70
Cocoa butter — 24
Colorful Cardinals — 77–78
Cookie cutters — 25
Cream cheese
    Chocolate Cream Cheese Frosting — 17

Cream Cheese Frosting — 17

D
Delightful Dreidels — 75
Dipping — 22–23
Dish towels — 25
Displays — 30–31
Double boilers — 20, 26
Dreidels, Delightful — 75

E
Elves, Freckled — 61–63
Equipment — 25–27, 30–31

F
Festive Pets — 85–86
Freckled Elves — 61–63
Friends, Frosty — 79–81

Frostings
    Buttercream Frosting — 17
    Chocolate Buttercream — 17
    Chocolate Cream Cheese Frosting — 17
    Cream Cheese Frosting — 17
    ready-made — 15, 24
Frosty Friends — 79–81

G
Gifts — 31
Gingerbread Houses — 71–73
Gingerheads — 35–36
Glassware — 30
Globes, Snow — 87–89

H
Holly, Jolly — 83
Houses, Gingerbread — 71–73

J

Jingle Bells   45

Jolly Holly   83

L

Lights, Bright   65

Lollipop sticks   26

Luster dust   25

M

Microwave   26

Mixers   26

Mixing bowls   26

O

Ornaments   67

P

Paramount crystals   25

Pens, edible-ink   24

Peppermint Pops   46

Pets, Festive   85–86

Polar Bears   49–50

Presents, Pretty   55

R

Red Velvet Cake   16–17

Reindeer, Red-Nosed   57

S

Santas   58–60

Shapes, creating   19–20

Shipping   31

Snowflakes, Simple   41

Snow Globes   87–89

Soldiers, Sweet   51–53

Spoons   26

Spray, edible   24

Sprinkles   25, 27–28

Squeeze bottles   26

Stockings, Stuffed   42

Styrofoam blocks   26, 30

Sweet Soldiers   51–53

T

Tags   31

Toothpicks   26–27

Trees, Cheery Christmas   69–70

Troubleshooting   13–14

Tweezers   27

W

Warming trays   21, 27

Wax paper   27

Wood displays   30–31

Wreaths, Welcoming   37–39

Y

Yellow Cake   15

Also available from Bakerella, creator of the original Cake Pops!

Cake Pops Kit · $19.95

Cake Pops · $19.95

The *New York Times* Bestseller; more than 800,000 in print!

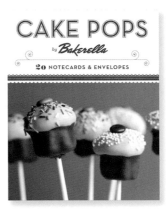

Cake Pops Notecards · $14.95